Building the First Pyramid: The History of the Ancient Egyptian Religious Beliefs and Archaeology Behind Djoser's Step Pyramid

By Charles River Editors

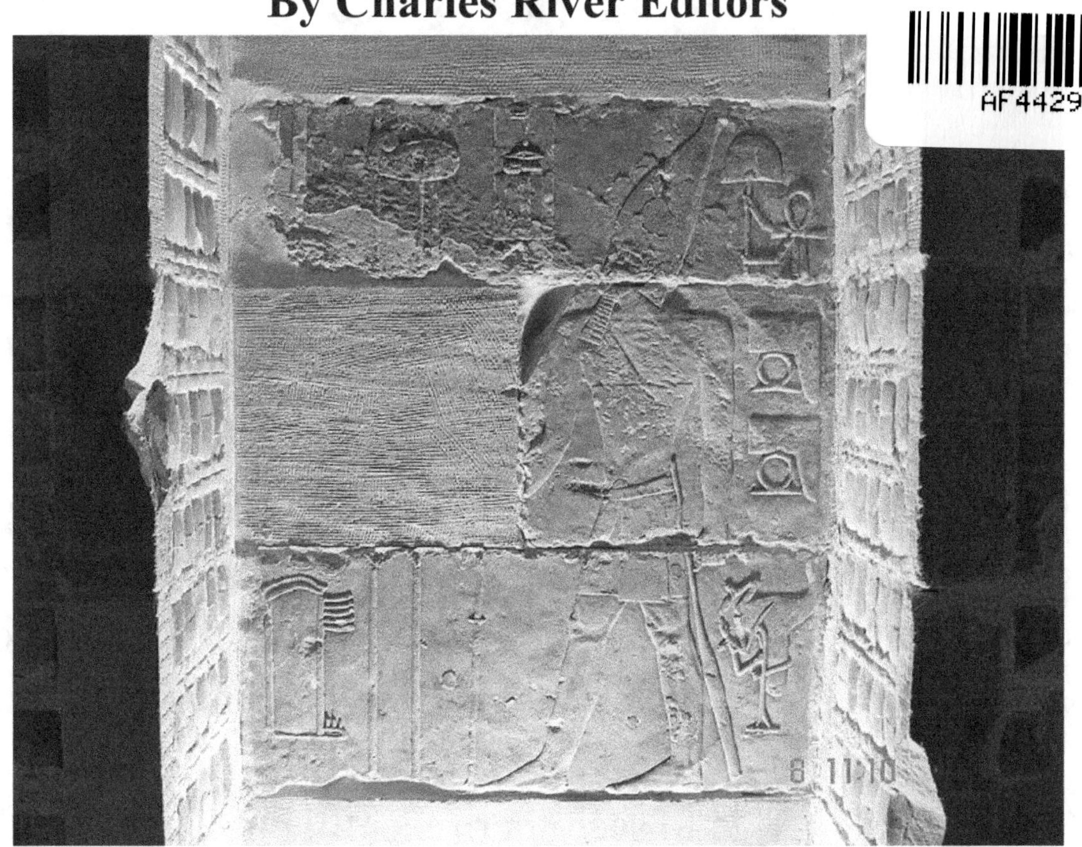

Juan R. Lazaro's picture of a relief inside the tomb of Djoser's Step Pyramid

Introduction

Charles J. Sharp's picture of Djoser's Step Pyramid

Africa may have given rise to the first human beings, and Egypt probably gave rise to the first great civilizations, which continue to fascinate modern societies across the globe nearly 5,000 years later. From the Library and Lighthouse of Alexandria to the Great Pyramid at Giza, the ancient Egyptians produced several wonders of the world, revolutionized architecture and construction, created some of the world's first systems of mathematics and medicine, and established language and art that spread across the known world. With world-famous leaders like King Tut and Cleopatra, it's no wonder that today's world has so many Egyptologists.

What makes the accomplishments of the ancient Egyptians all the more remarkable is that Egypt was historically a place of great political turbulence. Its position made it both valuable and vulnerable to tribes across the Mediterranean and the Middle East, and Egypt had no shortage of its own internecine warfare. Its most famous conquerors would come from Europe, with Alexander the Great laying the groundwork for the Hellenic Ptolemy line and the Romans extinguishing that line after defeating Cleopatra and driving her to suicide.

Perhaps the most intriguing aspect of ancient Egyptian civilization was its inception from the ground up, as the ancient Egyptians had no prior civilization which they could use as a template. In fact, ancient Egypt itself became a template for the civilizations that followed. The Greeks and the Romans were so impressed with Egyptian culture that they often attributed many attributes of their own culture–usually erroneously–to the Egyptians. With that said, some minor elements of ancient Egyptian culture were, indeed, passed on to later civilizations. Egyptian statuary appears to have had an initial influence on the Greek version, and the ancient Egyptian language continued long after the pharaonic period in the form of the Coptic language.

The pyramids of Egypt are such recognizable symbols of antiquity that for millennia, people have made assumptions about what they are and why they exist, without full consideration of the various meanings these ancient symbolic structures have had over the centuries.

Generations have viewed them as symbols of a lost past, which in turn is often portrayed as a world full of romance and mystery. This verbal meaning has become associated with the structures through the tourism industry, where intrigue obviously boosts ticket sales. In fact, the Egyptian pyramids are so old that they were also drawing tourists even in ancient times. In antiquity, the Great Pyramid of Giza was listed as one of Seven Ancient Wonders of the World, and it is the only one still surviving today.

The age and structural integrity of the pyramids also make them symbols of longevity and power, which is only fitting because those are two purposes the ancient pharaohs who commissioned these works intended them to serve. For the pharaohs, the construction of these large monuments presented an opportunity for them to showcase their influence and become something to be remembered by, both in the society they ruled and in the annals of history that would follow. Even as new dynasties came and went, and even as Egypt was subjected to foreign domination and rulers from across the world, the pyramids have continued to stand as a prominent testament to ancient Egypt's glorious past.

While the Great Pyramid of Giza is the most recognizable, the tradition of pyramid building was a long one in ancient Egypt occurring over hundreds of years, with techniques developing and improving, only to be forgotten and lost again. As a result, even as subsequent generations contributed new large-scale construction programs that changed the face of Egypt, they did so in quite different manners. The first of these was the Step Pyramid, located in the northwest of the city of Memphis in the Saqqara necropolis of Egypt. Today it is known as the Step Pyramid due to its stepped appearance, but in Egyptian times it was referred to as kbhw-ntrw. Commissioned by and made for the burial of the pharaoh Djoser, its design and construction was overseen by his vizier Imhotep. The name Imhotep has since become infused with popular culture through the popular series of Mummy movies, where the mummified remains of Imhotep are reanimated through the power of an ancient curse, leading to the shambling, linen-wrapped and decomposing undead monster haunting the hapless treasure seekers who dared disturb his resting place.[1] In reality, the ancient Imhotep was a talented architect and builder who succeeded in creating something that had never been seen before. It was a design that would often be repeated, even improved upon, and it gave birth to an ancient industry dedicated to the afterlife, one that would leave an indelible mark on Egyptian life as well as death.

---

[1] Sommers, Stephen. 1999. *The Mummy*. Universal Pictures, USA.

The Kingdoms of Ancient Egypt

The sun god Ra was considered by all ancient Egyptians as their first king, so religion and politics in Egypt were bound together, even from the earliest times. All major events were recorded using the specific year of a particular king's reign. This methodology is not without complications, however, and the exact dating of events has still proven problematic for modern historians. Manetho's 30 dynasties have been further sub-divided into "kingdoms," but there are periods when the social and political conditions were so chaotic it has proven impossible to determine who ruled what and when. These times are generally referred to as "Intermediate Periods."

The modern academic consensus now accepts the format that divides the history of ancient Egyptian into kingdoms and periods, beginning with the Archaic Period, starting around 3100 B.C. and lasting 414 years. This was followed by the Old Kingdom that existed for the next 505 years. The First Intermediate Period lasted for a total of 126 years, followed by the Middle Kingdom that covered the next 405 years. The Second Intermediate Period followed that, and it lasted 100 years before giving way to the New Kingdom, which lasted 481 years. The Third intermediate Period lasted 322 years, and the Late Period another 415 years. The final one was the Ptolemaic, which lasted 302 years.

The Archaic Period (3100 B.C.-2686 B.C.) included the

First Dynasty. Egyptian tradition held that the first human king, Menes (also known as Narmer), united the two separate lands that had existed before his time, bringing them together to create Egypt. There were seven kings in this First Dynasty, which ended in 2890 B.C. The Second Dynasty lasted from then until 2686 B.C. The First Dynasty appears to have ended following a period of strife over the succession that resulted in Hetepsekhemwy taking control, but he was never secure on the throne. The last ruler of the Second Dynasty, its fourth, was Khasekhemwy, who took a title meaning "arising in respect of the two powers," and "the two lords are at peace in him."[2] As with the First Dynasty, the Second ended in chaos and civil war.

The next major period following the Archaic was that of the Old Kingdom (2686 B.C.-2180 B.C.) and included the Third Dynasty. This dynasty lasted only a relatively short period (2686 B.C.-2613 B.C.), but it was one of enormous importance and widely regarded as a major watershed in world history. It was in this dynasty that the first pyramid, the Step Pyramid at Saqqara, appeared, as well as when so many of Egypt's other greatest artistic masterpieces were created. It was also during the reign of the Third Dynasty's greatest king, Djoser (*r.* 2667 B.C.-2648 B.C.), that Imhotep came to prominence and brought with him many of the innovations that shaped Egyptian history

---

[2] Clayton, 2006, p. 26

from then on.

The success of Third Dynasty rulers in maintaining peace and enriching Egypt laid the foundations for rulers of the Fourth Dynasty (2613 B.C.-2494 B.C.), during which time the Giza Pyramids were built, and Egyptian art reached even higher levels. It can be argued that Imhotep's direct influence was most obvious in that era, even though he was dead by that time. Sneferu and Khufu from the Fourth Dynasty are among the most renowned of all the pharaohs, and Imhotep's influence on their building projects is apparent. The transition from the Fourth to the Fifth Dynasties occurred without bloodshed, and Imhotep's impact can, again, be discerned in the religious practices he introduced becoming consolidated.

The Fifth Dynasty lasted from 2494 to 2345 B.C., and it is from this time that some of the best surviving papyri date. They provide invaluable information on accounting systems and demonstrate the sophisticated level Egyptian record-keeping had reached. This dynasty is particularly known for its mortuary temples and carvings, regarded as the pinnacle of Egyptian art, and where Imhotep's innovations in religious practices are most clearly evident.

The Sixth Dynasty (2345 B.C.-2181 B.C.) is famous for the number and quality of inscriptions dating to this time, including detailed records of trading expeditions to the south. The pyramid of Pepi II—one of the dynasty's rulers—at southern Saqqara is the last major monument of the Old Kingdom. There are no records whatsoever naming the kings of the Seventh Dynasty, and the Eighth Dynasty was one of political decay. The collapse of the Old Kingdom was accompanied by environmental disasters, causing devastating famines and the failure of the Nile to flood. Herodotus refers to Nitokris ruling at some point during the Intermediate Period: "She killed hundreds of Egyptians to avenge the king, her brother, whom his subjects had killed, and had forced her to succeed. She did this by constructing a huge underground chamber. Then invited to a banquet all those she knew to be responsible for her brother's death. When the banquet was underway, she let the river in on them through a concealed pipe. After this fearful revenge, she flung herself into a room filled with embers to escape her punishment."[3]

The next period in Egyptian history was totally confused, with one warlord after another trying to secure power. None succeeded, however, and the country was split into two once again. These two separate kingdoms—one in the north ruled from Herakeopolis, and one in the south ruled from Thebes—were in almost continuous conflict from then until the period of the Eleventh Dynasty (c. 2130 B.C.-c.1991 B.C.), when the country was united once again.

In assessing Imhotep's significance, it is important to

---

³ Herodotus, *Histories*, II, 100.

understand the period in which he lived, when his direct impact was most obvious. It also has to be recognized that his reputation continued many hundreds of years after his death and was probably at its height in the Eighteenth Dynasty (1549/1550 B.C.-1292 B.C.), and he continued to have a significant impact on Egyptian beliefs and culture right up to the time of his deification (525 B.C.), 2,000 years after his death. His deification enhanced his influence even further, and in the Roman Empire period, he was regarded as a major historical figure. However, the major contributions that occurred during his lifetime and at specific times during the ensuing eras were all dependent on the prevailing social, religious, and political situation, and it is in the Old Kingdom, Egypt's "Golden Age," when the Giza Pyramids were constructed that his greatest influence can be discerned.

Historians can find evidence for only a very small number of commoners that were deified, but the information is scant. Certainly, none achieved Imhotep's notoriety. The crucial question is: why and how did this non-royal personage acquire the status he did, and what, exactly, were the accomplishments that resulted in his being given the honor of being one of only two non-royal Egyptians known to have been deified?[4] The answer to this appears to lie more in the realm of the gods than in politics. Imhotep as a political figure was arguably no

---

[4] The other was Amenhotep, an architect and the son of Hapu (c. 1425 B.C.-c. 1356 B.C.).

more significant than many other officials who had served successful Pharaohs. Neither was he a particularly important military figure. The reasons behind his deification have to be sought in other areas. In Imhotep's case, the other sphere of Egyptian life in which he had such an impact was religion.

The Development of Egyptian Religion

From as early as the Early Dynastic Period, the country was divided into smaller dominions along the river that modern scholars call "Nomes". The word "nome" comes from the ancient Greeks who, during the rule of the Greek Ptolemaic Dynasty (332-30 BCE) in Egypt, referred to each as a kind of "pasturage" coming under the overarching rule of the Pharaoh of that kingdom. This made for a useful way of organizing the inhabitants of the two kingdoms, but it causes problems when trying to define what version of a common myth is the "correct" or "most widely believed". The reason for this is that the myths, though they had some similarities, could diverge widely from nome to nome. That is why writers such as the ancient historian Plutarch chose to single out a particular version of a myth and record or study it alone.

Later scholars further subdivided these various types of myth according to the cult center that either produced or "standardized" them.[5] They refer to them as "theologies," such as the "Memphite Theology" (myths from Memphis)

---

[5] Shaw 2015

or the "Heliopolitan Theology" (myths from Heliopolis). There is the theory that these "theologies" were competing in some way with others from different cult centers. Shaw, however, takes the view that they were more alternatives than opposing theories and although each cult center would substitute a god from another nome for one of their own local deities, there wasn't really any kind of animosity between the differing believers. Despite the fact that there was no externally enforced dogma over the whole of Egypt, the Egyptians still managed to maintain some overarching concepts. One such concept is that of the creation of the universe. Generally speaking, there was a limitless dark ocean of "chaos" called Nun, out of which a god was born who instigated creation.[6] The different cult centers felt at liberty to amend or augment that concept to incorporate local tastes and allegiances to deities. Later on, during the period of the New Kingdom, the cult center of Thebes gained prominence and the priests there tried to unify the earlier traditions of Egypt. In this attempt, Amun was the creator god but the Thebans also incorporated the traditions of the major cult centers like Hermopolis, Memphis and Heliopolis, which often seem quite disparate accounts to the modern reader but were quite ingeniously brought together at Thebes around 1200 BCE.[7]

---

[6] Shaw 2015
[7] Shaw 2015

The general creation story contains within it two aspects that are crucial to understanding all of the myths of ancient Egypt: *maat* and *isfet*. Isfet represents chaos or disorder, generally speaking, and it was seen as a fundamental element of everything in existence. There was no notion of trying to eradicate isfet from their general lives in ancient Egypt; after all, it was said to be one of the elements that was present in the limitless ocean at the dawn of creation. The only desire for ancient Egyptians was that isfet never became more prevalent than maat, its opposite: justice. Maat was often depicted as a goddess wearing a feather on her head, which was also the hieroglyph that represented her.[8] She, or simply the concept of justice, was believed to be present in all aspects of life and if it was broken by anyone, there would be a punishment. According to the Middle Kingdom *Coffin Texts* it was believed that Atum, the "Great Finisher" of creation,[9] inhaled maat in order to gain his consciousness: "Inhale your daughter Maat [said Nun to Atum] and raise her to your nostril so that your consciousness may live. May they not be far from you, your daughter Maat and your son Shu, whose name is "life" … it is your son Shu who will lift you up."[10]

After that, Atum was capable of making the waters of Nun recede away from him, making him rise above them

[8] Shaw 2015
[9] Shaw 2015
[10] 80 see Shaw 2015

and become "what remained" or the "mound of creation." It's important to take note of the fact that there was no creation until Atum inhaled life and justice. Therefore without maat and her dualistic counterpart, there would have been no world, and that is the reason for maat and isfet's ubiquity, as well as the acceptance of chaos in the world as seen by the ancient Egyptians. After Atum had separated himself from Nun, the children he kept inside, notably Shu and maat/isfet, often represented as a form of the goddess Tefnut, were now separated from their father, and Tefnut would go on to become the mother of all the gods.

   According to the acclaimed Egyptologist Garry Shaw, the Egyptian ethos was "an endless repetition of creations, destructions and rebirths, entangled in a net of divine interactions … each person [living] as the hero of his own mythic narrative each day."[11] In this way, the ancient Egyptians would "assimilate" themselves with the corresponding deity that defined their situation at any given time. Shaw gives an enlightening set of examples on this topic, writing, "A person with a headache became Horus the Child, cared for by his mother, who herself became Isis; in death, the deceased transformed into various gods whilst traversing the afterlife realm, assuming each deity's divine authority for a time. Egypt's myths were elastic enough to be shaped into everyone's

---

[11] Shaw 2015

lives … myths, and the acts of the gods detailed therein, answered the question, 'why did this happen to me?' There is comfort in precedent."[12]

Relating oneself to "Horus the Child" would have been of especial importance for the ancient Egyptian, centered as it is within the concept of the ubiquitous "Divine Mother." One of the functions of the character of "divine mother" in world mythology is to maintain the sentiment of protectiveness and caregiving in early religions. Her role in the religious mindset of early humans was initially a dominant one, but in the 9th and 8th millennia BCE, when the androcentric nomadic cultures finally joined with the goddess-exalting societies that had built the first manifestations of the human desire for companionship and protection, the more bellicose and "heroic" aspects of myth gained more religious prominence. To an ancient Egyptian, "becoming" Horus the Child was to find oneself in the protective embrace of the mother once more and to have the hope of convalescing and becoming stronger than before.

Horus's myth contributes to this religious mindset in two ways. On the one hand, Horus is the vanquishing hero of the divine royal line who epitomized "right" action and goodness over evil. On the other hand, he achieves that level of kingship only after being cared for as a sickly baby who was pursued by the evils of the world

____

[12] Ibid.

manifested by his uncle, Seth. This notion of assimilating oneself with Horus would have gone beyond mere semantic facility and would have given the believer a means of rationalizing the hostilities of the world around them. It also meant to inspire hope of finally vanquishing them and achieving adulthood and all the ambitions that came with it.

Every Egyptian was destined for eternity after death, but the Egyptians had no conception of an ethereal, otherworldly afterlife. Instead, the Egyptians believed that they would spend eternity in an eternal Egypt and that their lives there would mirror a perfect reflection of life as it had been lived in the Egypt of this earth. Eternal Egypt was known to the ancient Egyptians by a few different names. Most commonly, it was known as The Field of Reeds, but it was also commonly called Lily Lake and the Field of Plenty. Egyptian burial rites reflected this vision of eternity.

Scholars have established that the first Egyptian burial rites were practiced by 4000 BCE, and from that point until the Roman takeover of Egypt around 30 BCE, Egyptian burial rites demonstrated an unwavering focus on eternal life and the continuance of personal existence after death.[13]

---

[13] The ancient world was fascinated by the Egyptian burial, which became well known via cultural transmission through trade along the Silk Road. The Egyptian buran doubtless bore a great influenced on a number of other civilizations and religions—it was certainly a major source of inspiration for the Christian vision of eternal life.

Thus, Egyptian burial rites were very dramatic, even though Egyptians hoped that the deceased would find eternal bliss in the Field of Reeds. The ancient Greek historian Herodotus describes these dramatic rites: "As regards mourning and funerals, when a distinguished man dies, all the women of the household plaster their heads and faces with mud, then, leaving the body indoors, perambulate the town with the dead man's relatives, their dresses fastened with a girdle, and beat their bared breasts. The men too, for their part, follow the same procedure, wearing a girdle and beating themselves like the women. The ceremony over, they take the body to be mummified."[14]

At a very early point in the history of their civilizations, the Egyptians seem to have developed the concept of an eternal soul, and it was believed that the entire[15] body of the deceased needed to be preserved on Earth in order for that soul to be able to enjoy an eternal afterlife. Even those Egyptians who couldn't afford to pay anything at all were given some kind of burial, as it was believed that the souls of the deceased who had not been properly buried would return as a ghost and spend eternity haunting the living.[16]

---

[14] (Nardo, 110)

[15] ancient Egyptians believed that the soul consisted of nine separate parts. The physical body was known as the *Khat*; the *Ka* was one's double form; the *Ba* was a human headed bird aspect which was able to speed between earth and the heavens; *Shuyet* was the shadow self; *Akh* was the immortal, transformed self; *Sahu* and *Sechem* were aspects of the *Akh*; *Ab* was the heart, which was the source of good and evil; *Ren* was one's secret name. Without the *Ka* and the *Ba*, the *Khat* was believed to be unable to recognize itself.

[16] The return of a ghost was considered to be a very serious matter, as the Egyptians were not able to

These beliefs gave rise to the practice of mummification, by far the most well-known aspect of the Egyptian burial practices. Mummification in ancient Egypt has almost as long a history as any religious ritual in the culture, and it is likely that the first Egyptian mummies were somewhat accidental. Predynastic burials were often placed in desert areas, where the grave's hot, dry sand absorbed the corpse's fluids and preserved the body.[17] After this, the people of ancient Egypt began to actively experiment with ways to preserve the body. One factor may have been a general move away from the pit grave in the desert to deeper graves with brick- or wood-lined burial chambers or coffins, which stopped natural mummification.[18] In addition to this, the Egyptians strove to perfect the process of preserving the body, making it truly last for an eternity.

---

tolerate the idea of non-existence. If the deceased was not given a proper burial (or if their loved ones had committed some sin before or after death), the gods gave the *Akh* dispensation to return to earth in order to redress the wrong. The Akh would then harass the living, who would have to plead their case to the ghost in the hopes of receiving a reasonable response. If they were not able to receive one themselves, a priest would have to intervene and serve as arbiter between the living and the dead. If, for example, misfortune were to befall a widower, that misfortune would first be attributed to some "sin" he had committed against his wife, who, omniscient in the Field of Reeds, was now punishing him. One such widower wrote a letter to his dead wife, begging her to leave him alone and insisting that he was innocent of any wrong-doing. The letter, which he delivered to her in her tomb, reads as follows: "What wicked thing have I done to you that I should have come to this evil pass? What have I done to you? But what you have done to me is to have laid hands on me although I had done nothing wicked to you. From the time I lived with you as your husband down to today, what have I done to you that I need hide? When you began to grow sick from the illness which you had, I caused a master-physician to be fetched...I spent eight months without eating and drinking like a man. I wept exceedingly together with my household in front of my street-quarter. I gave linen clothes to wrap you and left no benefit undone that had to be performed for you. And now, behold, I have spent three years alone without entering into a house, though it is not right that one like me should have to do it. This have I done for you sake. But, behold, you do not know good from bad." (Nardo, 32).

[17] Taylor 2001, 46

[18] Taylor 2001, 47

As that indicates, mummification became about so much more than just preserving the body. The process itself was an important ritual, as the body had to undergo specific and special treatment for it to serve as an eternal image of the deceased. Ritual treatment of corpses had already begun in the predynastic, and around 3500 BCE, corpses in Hierakonpolis were wrapped in hides or linen. Resin and linen padding were already being used to transform corpses into the ideal bodies, and by the First Dynasty, linen wrappings were used regularly on the dead.[19]

As with the development of most things in ancient Egypt, there were multiple ideas and traditions coexisting at the same time. In other words, what would become the standard version of mummification was not always the only option. In the late predynastic period, some areas of Egypt began to dismember corpses of the deceased and allow the corpse to decompose, after which the bones would be put back together. Inevitably, however, the individuals putting the bones back together did not always have the best knowledge of anatomy, so some of the bones were reassembled out of place. There are some examples of this treatment in late predynastic period graves at Naqada and Adaima. There are also some examples through the end of the Old Kingdom, but during this period, the treatment was rare and restricted to higher status individuals.[20]

---

[19] Taylor 2001, 46

Other than these few examples, dismemberment was seen as something to avoid when dealing with the bodies of the deceased, as it had the ability to ward off potential harm inflicted against the living by the deceased and was thus interpreted as acting as somewhat of a punishment. That said, a connection to the deity Osiris, god of the underworld, may have made it more favorable for some. In the most common myth, Osiris is murdered and his body was dismembered by his brother Seth. Reconstructing the corpse and turning it into a mummy thus became a metaphor for surviving death. This version of rites, which involves dismembering the body and rejoining the bones, mirrored the myth of Osiris in which the deceased becomes the god himself, as in the *Pyramid Texts*.[21]

The myths may have arrived at the hands of scholars from inscriptions on pyramid walls (such as the Old Kingdom's *Pyramid Texts*), painted on the inside of coffins (such as the Middle Kingdom's *Coffin Texts*), or texts written on papyri (such as the famous "Book of the Dead," which dates back to the Second Intermediate Period).[22] The mythologist's job is made even more

---

[20] Taylor 2001, 47-48. Old Kingdom examples found at Giza, Meidum, and Deshasha, the latest being dated to the 6th dynasty.

[21] *Pyramid Texts*, along with later texts such as the *Coffin Texts* and the *Book of the Dead*, can refer to the deceased as Osiris himself or "Osiris [name]," using the god's name as a title for the honored dead. For example, see Allen's spell 199a, which reads: "Recitation. Ho, Osiris Teti! Geb has fetched Horus for you, that he might tend you. He has fetched you the gods' hearts, that you might not groan, that you might not moan. Horus has given you his eye, that you might acquire the crown in it at the fore of the gods. Horus has gathered your limbs for you and joined you, and nothing of you can be disturbed. Thoth has seized your opponent for you, beheaded along with his retinue, and there was none of them whom he spared" (Allen, 2015, p. 82)

[22] Shaw 2015

exacting by the fact that, since the scribes who documented the myths assumed their readers were knowledgeable about the stories' details, they opted to refer to myths obliquely out of a sense of decorum. This was often the case for Osiris, whose death was a troublesome topic for those inscribing on the funerary monuments since it was thought that simply mentioning his death could "magically harm the deceased."[23]

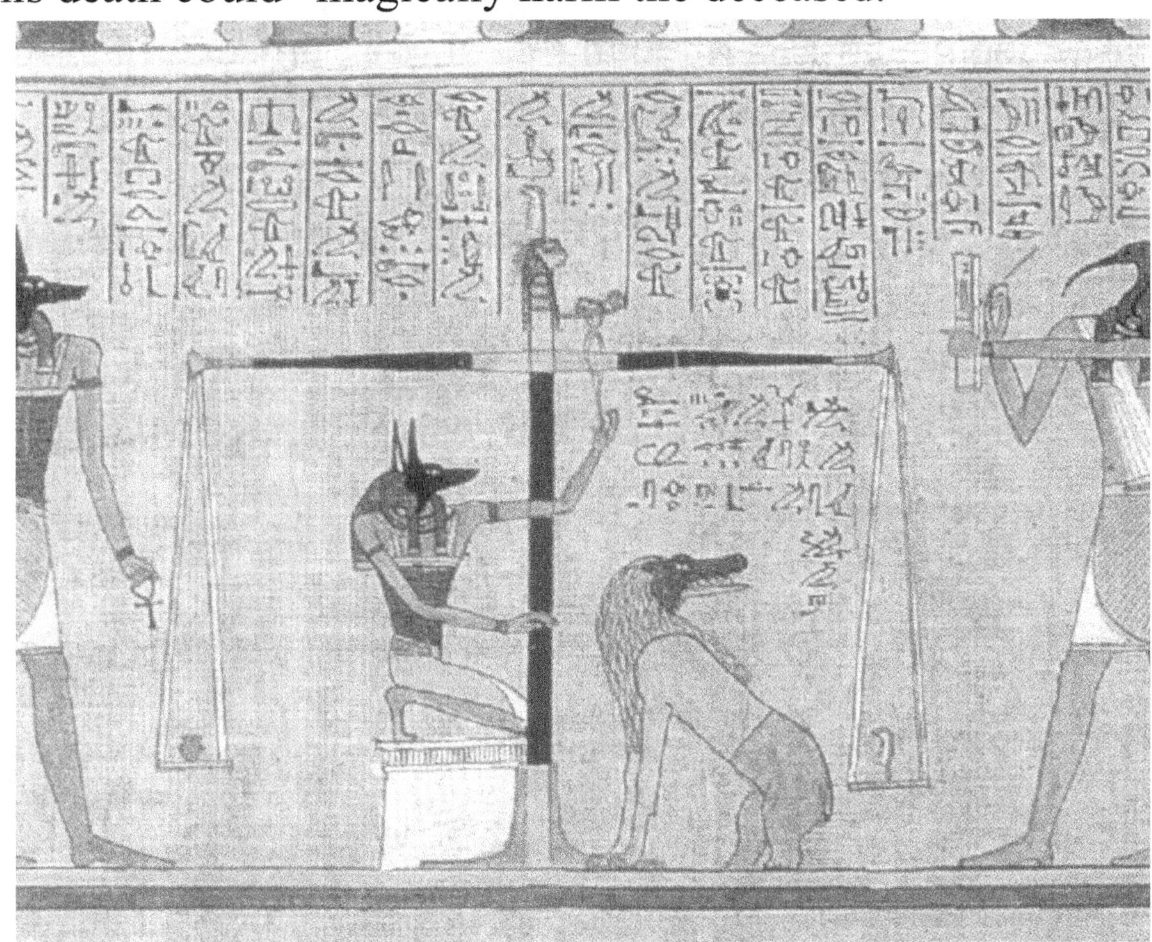

[23] Shaw 2015

Scenes from the *Book of the Dead*

The vast history of Egypt makes tracking the development of certain myths a complex process. In terms of the oldest description of death, modern scholars have the *Pyramid Texts*. These were initially inscribed on the walls of the Fifth Dynasty pyramid of Unas at Saqqara,[24] and they documented and gave advice to the king on his journey into the afterlife. These inscriptions were later copied onto other pyramids from the Old Kingdom and have therefore survived in good condition.

---

[24] Shaw 2015

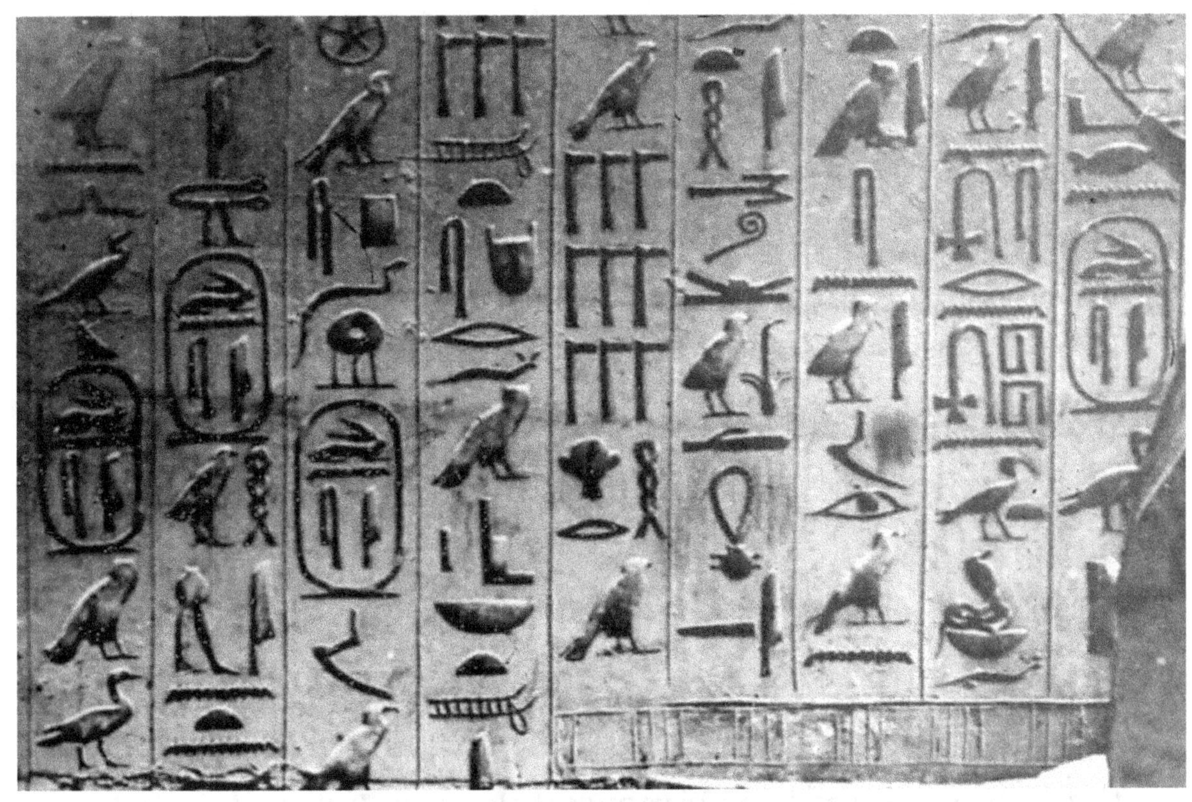

Unas *Pyramid Texts*

After dismemberment was abandoned, mummification focused on making the corpse as perfect as it could be. This eternal image of the deceased was called a *sAḥ*, and the new body was imbued with magical attributes. The word *sAḥ* comes from the s causative + *Aḥ*, with an *Aḥ* being an honored dead spirit. These spirits were considered very powerful, even able to influence the lives of the living.[25] The body was not meant to look exactly as it had in life but rather as a perfect image.[26] From this period onward, mummification was standard for anyone who could afford it.

While the first mummies were likely accidental, with the

[25] For a more detailed discussion of this term, see Janák 2013.
[26] Taylor 2001, 48

hot, dry sand preserving the body, as time went on, the process of intentional mummification became more regulated. The word "mummy" comes from the Persian "*mummia*," for bitumen. The word, "embalming," on the other hand, comes from the Latin "*in balsamum*," meaning "to preserve through the agency of balm." The word "mummy" was often used due to an association of the dark appearance of a mummy with the substance of bitumen, despite the fact it was not used in mummification until the New Kingdom, and even then it was not widely used. In fact, bitumen was not regularly used in mummification until the Late Period. Before that, the skin of mummies appeared dark as a result of the use of resin.[27]

The first step in mummification was to thoroughly wash the body. This was not only for purification purposes, but because decomposition would begin quickly, so washing also served a practical purpose. It is likely that a solution of water and natron was used for preliminary body cleaning.[28]

Next, certain organs were removed. This, too, was partially practical, because internal organs decompose and spread decomposition throughout the body if not removed quickly. The brain was extracted through the nose, and to accomplish this, the roof of the nasal cavity was

---

[27] Taylor 2001, 47
[28] Taylor 2001, 51-53

perforated with a small chisel or awl, after which a metal hook was used to break up and extract the brain. They could also extract the brain through the eye socket or a hole in the cranium or base of the skull. The brain was seen as little more than stuffing for the skull in ancient Egypt, since the Egyptians believed the power of thought and consciousness lay in the heart. After the brain was removed, the skull was packed with linen cloth, sawdust, or occasionally, molten resin.[29]

After the brain, the main organs, including the liver, lungs, stomach, and intestines, were removed, embalmed separately, and placed in canopic jars. The significance of this will be discussed further below, and the kidneys were sometimes removed as well but were more often left inside the body. The heart was always intentionally left in the body because it was believed the deceased would need it in the afterlife. According to Herodotus, embalmers sometimes did not remove the organs but injected "oil of cedar"[30] into the body through the rectum instead. He wrote that this was to dissolve the organs, but the true intent may have been to preserve the organs within the body. After the organs were removed, the interior of the body was washed. Herodotus explained that this was done with both water and palm wine.[31]

The next step involved drying out the corpse. This was

---

[29] Taylor 2001, 53
[30] Possibly juniper oil, but this would not dissolve the organs as described.
[31] See Taylor, 2001, 53-56 in addition to the original text of *The Histories* by Herodotus.

also practical in that removing liquids from the body stopped bacteria, which caused decay. The most common way to dry out the body was with natron, a compound of salts famously found at the Wadi Natrun. There were, however, many sources, and the chemical composition varied. One ancient Egyptian term for the substance[32] was *ntri* (netjery), meaning something akin to "divine substance." This term is thought to be the source of the modern term for the substance and the Latin *"natrium,"* which gives sodium its chemical abbreviation of "Na." Natron was particularly effective for drawing moisture out of the corpse in addition to being useful in breaking down fatty tissues. The salts were usually used as a powder,[33] with linen packages of natron being stuffed inside the body cavity. The body was covered in natron powder and allowed to rest for a period of time, usually approximately 40 days.[34] During this time, the natron absorbed all fluids in the body.

After that, the natron was removed from the body, and by this time, most of the muscles and fat would have disappeared, leaving mainly the skeleton and skin. The body cavities were then rinsed and filled to give the body a more lifelike appearance, and these packing materials were often scented with aromatic resins to provide a more pleasant smell. The main packing materials were linen,

---

[32] The more common ancient Egyptian term was *hsmn.*

[33] Taylor 2001, 55-56

[34] Herodotus mentioned seventy days but was likely describing the entire mummification process. Egyptian texts often mention seventy days as the time period between death and burial.

sawdust, and dirt, but in later periods and during the Roman occupation, mummies were often filled with molten resin.

For example, by the Third Intermediate Period, packing material was also placed under the skin in an attempt to restore a more lifelike appearance. The exterior of the body was then anointed with oils and perfumes, while resins were often used at this stage for the aromatic qualities, providing some "suppleness" to the limbs and protecting the body from moisture.[35] Bitumen was sometimes used in addition to (or instead of) resin, although usually only in later periods.

The body was then carefully attended to with respect to cosmetic matters. The hair was done, false eyes were added, and features such as eyebrows were painted on. In the same vein, missing limbs were given false substitutes to complete the full-body image. After all that was complete, the mummy was then wrapped in linen, often reused from households, with the head and limbs wrapped individually before the entire body was wrapped together. Sometimes, linen was added to the wrappings to fill out the corpse to a more standard mummy shape.[36]

The external appearance of mummies was extremely important, as this was what created the perfect image, but even this image looked different in different periods. In

---

[35] Taylor 2001, 57
[36] Taylor 2001, 58-59

the Old Kingdom, resin-soaked linen or plaster was used to create a statue-like appearance. The limbs were kept separate from the body, and the body was dressed in clothing. From the First Intermediate Period onward, the limbs were confined within the wrappings, looking more like the classic image of the mummified Osiris. Next, the head was often covered in a mask with an idealized image of the deceased. The bodies were then treated with molten resin, which may have been considered to give the deceased a divine status. Occasionally, bodies were treated with beeswax, which had associations with rebirth.[37]

[37] Taylor 2001, 48-49

**A statue of Osiris showing him wrapped in a pose
mimicked by mummies**

As the exterior was more important when creating the perfect image, the interior of the mummy was not as perfectly preserved. Some upper-class mummies, particularly the royal mummies of the New Kingdom, received better treatment, but today, mummy wrappings often only contain the bones of the deceased. The Third Intermediate Period was the exception to this trend, when embalmers experimented with ways to restore the corpse and replicate the appearance of the deceased in life.[38]

Various rituals were performed as the body was being wrapped. Some clothes placed on the body were given specific ritual names and could only be placed a certain way, and during this wrapping, amulets were strategically placed at specific points on the body. The locations of these amulets were clearly important, and Late Period and Ptolemaic funerary papyri showed the layout of where the amulets should be placed on the body.[39] Jewelry was also placed on the body during wrapping, including collars, earrings, bracelets, and finger rings, and since these were usually made of gold, silver, or other precious stones, mummies were often torn apart by thieves looking for valuable items.

A large outer shroud covered the entire body from head to foot in the last stage of wrapping. In the New Kingdom and Third Intermediate Period, this final shroud was dyed a reddish pink, perhaps in connection with the solar deity.[40]

---

[38] Taylor 2001, 48-49
[39] Andrews 1994, 7-9
[40] Taylor 2001, 59-60

Marco Almbauer's picture of a painted mummy bandage

Edoard Toda's picture of the Nesi mummy from the 20th Dynasty

As noted above, after the wrappings, in the Old Kingdom clothing would have been placed on the mummy. After the Old Kingdom, the corpse was wrapped as a whole, and the main adornment was a mask placed over the mummy's head. The most famous of these masks is that of King Tutankhamun from the 18th Dynasty. This mask was not usually designed as a portrait but rather as an effort to further the mummy's divine image. The mask also ensured the senses remained intact, with the eyes, mouth, nose, and ears represented, thus magically present for the deceased. Since the new ideal image of the mummy was a divine one, the mask often represented the skin of the gods using gold. Similarly, the hair was represented as blue lapis. As only the truly rich could afford these materials, substitutes were often made from cartonnage and painted.[41]

From the 25th Dynasty to the Ptolemaic Period, a beaded net of blue-green faience tubular beads was placed over the deceased. The bead nets had connections to Osiris and Isis and Nephthys as protectors of the deceased. During the Roman period, the last outer shroud of wrapping could also have a full-length image of the deceased.[42]

Once the corpse had been mummified, it was time for the funeral. The ancient Egyptians believed that the remembrance of the dead by the living ensured that the dead would continue to exist in the Field of Reeds. A great show of grief was thought to resound in the Hall of

---

[41] Taylor 2001, 61-63
[42] Taylor 2001, 63

Truth (or Hall of Osiris)—the first major destination of the deceased in the afterlife. Thus, the funeral was both an occasion to mourn the loss of the deceased and an occasion to celebrate and honor his life. Regardless of how popular the deceased may have been in life, it was traditional to have a group of professional mourners, called Kites, accompanying the funeral procession and burial. The Kites were paid to lament loudly throughout these proceedings, and traditionally, they would sing the "Lamentation of Isis and Nephthys," a lamentation song that had its origins in the myth of the two goddesses weeping over the death of Osiris. The song of the Kites was meant to inspire the other mourners at the funeral to show their emotion.

At some point prior to the funeral procession or immediately before placing the mummy in the tomb, a priest would perform the Opening of the Mouth Ceremony. This ceremony underscored the importance of the physical body; its purpose was to reanimate the corpse so that the immortal soul could continue to use it. In this ceremony, a priest recited spells while using a ritual blade to touch the mouth of the corpse—the touch of the blade was believed to enable the corpse to regain its ability to breathe, eat, and drink. Next, he touched the corpse's arms and legs so that it would be free to move about within the tomb (and beyond).

An ancient Egyptian mural depicting the opening the mouth ceremony

**A mural depicting the Opening of the Mouth
ceremony for Tutankhamun**

After the body was at last laid to rest, the tomb was
sealed. Finally, the priest recited a number of other spells
and prayers, usually the Litany of Osiris, and if the
deceased was a pharaoh, the priest would recite a set of
spells from the *Pyramid Texts*. With this recitation, the
burial was complete, and the deceased was left to begin
his journey to the Field of Reeds.

The first "mummies" in Egypt were accidental, and
before the dynasties, burials were generally in shallow pits
in the desert sand with the corpse in a fetal position,

sometimes wrapped in matting or hides and usually buried directly in the sand. The hot desert sand would then absorb all moisture, leaving the skin, bones, hair, nails, and organs preserved. Later, in the 4th millennium BCE, basket trays and simple wooden box coffins were used to house the body, and the pit dug for burial became more elaborate with vertical sides and a wooden roof, measures that stopped the sand from taking its full effect on the body. The elite, especially, used these newer, more elaborate forms of burial.

In 3500 BCE, at Hierakonpolis, bodies were wrapped in linen and padded, perhaps to imitate the body's shape in life, and resin was being experimented with as a preservative agent. The bodies discovered there have not been tested for natron, but there is no evidence of evisceration.[43] Early dynastic burials often wrapped the bodies in linen, with each limb wrapped separately.[44] As mentioned above, some bodies from this period were dismembered and the dry bones were wrapped later.

During the Old Kingdom, more elaborate mummification treatments were restricted to the royal family and the elite. Add to this the high rate of tomb-robbing, and very few mummies from this period have survived. From the bodies that have been recovered, we see that the viscera were already being removed during mummification, although

---

[43] Ikram and Dodson 1998, 109

[44] Taylor 2001, 79. An arm of King Djer (1st dynasty) was discovered at Abydos with linen wrappings (Petrie, 1900, p. 16).

the brain was left intact. The corpse was laid out in an extended fashion, beginning in the 3rd Dynasty, when full-length coffins started to be made. The bodies from this period were not well-preserved due to the early stages of skill refinement and emphasis on the body's exterior over preservation of the interior. Linen padding was used to shape the body, and each limb was individually modeled. Some mummies from the 5th and 6th Dynasties show evidence of a plaster coating on the outer wrappings, which could be painted,[45] Though this was often only on the head and may have been the predecessor of mummy masks. Clothing was also put over the mummy's wrappings, used to make its appearance more lifelike.

Imhotep and the Design of the Pyramids

Imhotep lived during the Third Dynasty (c. 2670 B.C.-2613 B.C.), regarded as part of the Old Kingdom rather than the Early Dynastic Period primarily because of the many major building projects completed at the time. The most important of these was the first pyramid that was constructed during Djoser's reign.[46] There is, however, some disagreement between modern scholars, with some arguing that the Third Dynasty more logically belongs to the Early Dynastic Period because of what they perceive was a discernible continuity in religious practices and architectural methodology.

---

[45] Taylor 2001, 79

[46] Also spelt Djeser or Zoser. In Hellenic times, he was known as Tosorthros (see Manetho, *Aegyptiaca* (*History of Egypt*) and Sesorthos (from Eusebius, *Works*).

Wherever the dynasty should be placed, it was undoubtedly a very special time due to the construction of the first major pyramid at Saqqara, and there is no academic dispute as to whether Imhotep designed the pyramid.[47] The debate as to whether the design is more a development of the *mastaba* tombs of the Early Dynastic Period than the forerunner of the well-known pyramids of the Fourth Dynasty of the Old Kingdom is, however, still taking place. What is certain is that it was in the Third Dynasty that single-story mastabas were redesigned into what some call the stacked mastabas of the Step Pyramids of Djoser, Sekhemkhet, and Khaba.

---

[47] Bard, 2008, pp. 128-133

An ancient statuette of Imhotep, credited with designing the pyramid

The origins of the pyramids, including their chosen shape and design, stretch all the way back to the mythological stories of the ancient Egyptians. As a culture, the Egyptians are known for their obsession with death, so it is ironic that these lavish tombs were inspired instead by a story of creation – the story of birth.[48] In Egyptian mythology, the world was formed from out of

48 Rosenberg, Donna. 1986. *World Mythology*. HARRAP, Great Britain. pp 166-177.

the depths of a primal ocean that was both infinite and bereft of life, and these ancient waters parted when the sun rose for the very first time. This origin was something that the Egyptians referred to as the "first occasion". The chaotic waters of the lifeless ocean, an entity that they called Nu, parted as a pyramid shaped mound rose up through the waves. This shape, the benben, was the first part of Earth, the first sign of life, rising from out of the waters. The mythological imagery of Egypt naturally reflected the reality of their environment, where the rising waters of the Nile flooded the land, only to recede again and leave fertile ground with rich muds ready to be seeded with crops, the source of Egypt's bounty and life.[49]

While the shape of the pyramid derives from mythology, the Egyptians had several reasons for building them. The pyramids served religious and funerary purposes, while also serving as reinforcing power structures for Egypt's rulers, but the process of building also served a valuable practical function. Egypt required a large work force to produce the food needed to feed its people, as the rich soils surrounding the Nile needed to be seeded, crops tended and harvests reaped. For one entire season out of the year, however, the farming belt of Egypt was covered by water as the Nile flooded its banks, leading to a large part of Egypt's population being idle during that time. The building of monuments was a valuable method of keeping

<hr>

[49] Leeming, David Adams. 2010. *Creation Myths of the World*. AB.C.-CLIO, Santa Barbaro. pp 102.

an otherwise idle population active, thereby guaranteeing employment for all throughout the year. Farmers in the Old Kingdom period who were idle and wanted to work during the Nile's period of inundation could get paid and avoid taxes by working on pyramid building projects. Egyptian citizens with nothing to occupy them while their farming lands were under water could thus spend the season erecting timeless monuments to their ruler, receiving wine and beer thrice daily as part of their working conditions.[50]

Given the difficult and no doubt deadly nature of the labor, it has long been assumed that the Egyptians wouldn't have resorted to building the pyramids all by themselves. Popular culture images of present day have shown erroneous depictions of Jewish slaves being whipped as they dutifully push vast blocks of sandstone along on trundling wooden logs. Such was the case in *The Ten Commandments*[51] and the animated *Prince of Egypt* even showed wooden scaffolding around the Sphinx.[52] In reality, wood was a rare commodity in Egypt, imported from abroad and used as a prestige item. The Sudan supplied ebony wood, pine and cedar were imported from Syria,[53] and large timbers were imported from Lebanon

---

[50] Seawright, Caroline. 2013. *Egypt: The Nile Inundation*. Site accessed 4 September 2013.
http://www.touregypt.net/featurestories/nile.htm
[51] DeMille, Cecil B (director). 1956. *The Ten Commandments*. Paramount Pictures, USA.
[52] Chapman, Brenda; Hickner, Steve; Wells, Simon (directors). 1998. *The Prince of Egypt*. Dreamworks Pictures, USA.
[53] Egyptian Government. 2013. *Egypt: Trees in Egypt*. Site accessed 4 September 2013.
http://www.touregypt.net/featurestories/trees.htm

for shipbuilding.[54] The lack of wood in the largely desert regions of Egypt led fringe theorist Erich von Daniken to conclude that aliens must have been behind the construction of these great edifices, an explanation that has since had its own impact in popular culture through television programs like *Doctor Who*[55], as well as film and television franchises like *Stargate*.[56] "The stone blocks used for building," von Daniken stated, "were moved on rollers. In other words, wooden rollers! But the Egyptians would scarcely have felled and turned into rollers the few trees, mainly palms, that then (as now) grew in Egypt, because the dates from the palms were urgently needed for food and the trunks and fronds were the only things giving shade to the dried up ground. But they must have been wooden rollers, otherwise there would not even be the feeblest technical explanation of the building of the pyramids."[57]

Von Daniken's central argument about the achievements of the past is that humans did not have the capacity to attain such successes and were therefore not responsible for the great monuments of antiquity. He suggested instead a utopian past when space travelers, possibly native Martians seeking to escape changing environmental condition on their own world, escaped to Earth and

[54] Brier, Bob. 2007. How to Build a Pyramid. In: Archaeological Institute of America. 2007. *Archaeology Volume 60 Number 3, May/June 2007*. Archaeological Institute of America, USA.
[55] Russell, Paddy (director). 1975. *Doctor Who: Pyramids of Mars*. BB.C., UK.
[56] Emmerich, Roland (director). 1994. *Stargate*. Canal, USA.
[57] von Daniken, Erich. 1972. *Chariots of the Gods? Was God an Astronaut?* Gorgi, Great Britain. pp 97.

brought a wealth of knowledge and technology along with them.[58] Von Daniken theorized that "a group of Martian giants perhaps escaped to Earth to found the new culture of homo sapiens by breeding with the semi-intelligent beings living there… giants who come from the stars, who could move enormous blocks of stone, who instructed men in arts still unknown on Earth and who finally died out."[59]

However, experimental archaeology has come about as a profession to try to figure out the feasibility of these kinds of building projects by using reconstructive approaches that used the known building conditions and experiences of the past. Archaeological experiments found that while wood was in short supply, one thing that Egypt had plenty of during the time of the Nile inundation was mud. Using mud bricks to shape mud ramps, it was possible for limestone blocks to be pushed and hauled along the slippery surface of the wet ramps. Such experiments have even been used to estimate the building period times for pyramid construction. Although not conclusive in proving the methods of the past, they certainly demonstrate the possibilities that past Egyptian craftsmen could have used.[60] Another theory is that the process of building was split between an inner and outer ramp. While the outer ramp

---

[58] von Daniken, Erich. 1972. *Chariots of the Gods? Was God an Astronaut?* Gorgi, Great Britain. pp 99.

[59] von Daniken, Erich. 1972. *Chariots of the Gods? Was God an Astronaut?* Gorgi, Great Britain. pp 155.

[60] Lehner, Mark. 1997. *The Complete Pyramids*. Thames and Hudson, Slovenia.

was removed, the inner ramp became part of the pyramid's structure.[61]

Imhotep took a number of roles in his life. He was the high priest of an ancient Egyptian sun cult, chief counselor to the Pharaoh, an accomplished sculptor and an architect. He improved upon the existing funerary design of the mastaba by building mastabas of dwindling size each on top of the other. When it was finished, he had produced a stairway to heaven upon which the Pharaoh Djoser could ascend into the next life.[62]

---

[61] Brier, Bob. 2007. How to Build a Pyramid. In: Archaeological Institute of America. 2007. *Archaeology Volume 60 Number 3, May/June 2007*. Archaeological Institute of America, USA.
[62] Time Life Books. 1987. *The Age of God-Kings*. Time Life Books Inc, Amsterdam. pp 60.

A mastaba

Initially, only the highest officials and royalty were buried in mastabas. The term itself comes from the Arabic word for "a bench of mud," but it is not entirely clear where the design of the structures originated.[63] It may be that the Egyptians simply copied similar structures built in Mesopotamia at the time. Mastabas were rectangular, with sides sloping inwards and a flat roof. Some later mastabas were built of stone, but the most important continued to be built from sun-dried mud. They were normally four times as long as they were wide and approximately 30 feet in height. All of them were built on a north-south axis as ancient Egyptians believed that access to the afterlife could not be gained in any other way.

The actual burial chambers were lined with wood and cut into the rock. A second chamber, called a *serdab,* was built to accommodate the worldly goods the deceased were thought to need in the afterlife—these included items such as clothes, food, drink, and household items. A special statue of the deceased was made to protect the mastaba, hidden somewhere in the structure. Small openings in the serdab were cut to enable the *Ba* (a principal aspect of the soul for ancient Egyptians) to leave the mastaba and return to the statue, which took the place of the body. The holes were used by priests or family members to burn incense that could reach the dead

---

[63] Gardiner, 1964, p. 57

entombed inside.

The mastaba became the normal tomb for both the pharaoh and members of the social elite, with many of them built at Abydos,[64] while the royal cemetery was located at Saqqara just outside of Memphis. Even after pharaohs began constructing pyramids, the nobility appears to have continued their tradition of being buried in mastabas. Evidence for this comes, for example, from the Giza Plateau, where at least 150 mastaba tombs have been discovered alongside the pyramids.[65] Given their use over such prolonged periods, it is no surprise that the design of mastabas has changed over the centuries. During the First Dynasty, they were built to resemble houses and included a number of rooms, with the central one housing the sarcophagus. They came to be built over pits, but in the Second and Third Dynasties, the stairway mastaba was developed. In these types of mastabas, the chamber in which the tomb was located was much farther below ground level and was reached by a stairway.

Developments in the Fourth Dynasty (2613 B.C.-2494 B.C.) included rock-cut tombs built into rock cliffs in Upper Egypt, again, to try to prevent grave robbers from plundering the tombs. Offering chapels and vertical shafts were also added. In the Fifth Dynasty, these chapels became highly ornate, often consisting of several rooms,

---

[64] Located around seven miles west of the Nile, near the modern towns of El Araba Madfuna and El Balyana.
[65] Davis, 1997, *pp.89–92*

halls, and serdabs, with the tomb chamber being built below the south end of the mastaba itself. The slanting passage led to a stairway that exited into the hall. However, by the time of the New Kingdom, around 1550 B.C., the mastaba had declined in popularity, and pyramid chapels above a burial chamber became the norm.[66]

The Step Pyramid was crafted using cut stone construction, with the large steps decreasing in size as they rose in height, and the pyramid originally reached a total height of approximately 200 feet. Although currently appearing in the natural colors of the worn materials used in its construction, the pyramid was originally clad in limestone that was polished bright white, thus shining like a beacon under the bright light of Egypt's sun. Around it, a mortuary complex was built with various decorated structures for ceremony and religious rituals.[67]

---

[66] Badawy, 1966, p. 51
[67] Time Life Books. 1987. *The Age of God-Kings*. Time Life Books Inc, Amsterdam. Pp 62-63.

Temples near the complex

While it now looks old and has been surpassed by the pyramids that came after it, it is important to remember that at the time of its construction, the Step Pyramid was not only brand new but unlike anything Egyptians had ever seen. The Step Pyramid was radically different from the pre-existing architecture of Egypt, as were the techniques used to make it. While mud brick had previously been used for building practices, this cut stone edifice was much more labor intensive. It would also prove to have much greater longevity as a result. For centuries, the Step Pyramid dominated the landscape in which it was situated, due not only to its imposing size but also the shining white exterior that made it stand out all the more.

The exact date of construction for the Step Pyramid is not known, but it was built sometime during the reign of Pharaoh Djoser, who was estimated to have reigned for approximately 19 years between 2667-2648 B.C. The name Djoser is a modern one attributed to him, much as the Step Pyramid has been named long after the fact. In his tomb, he is referred to by his Horus name Netjerykhet.[68] Ruler during Egypt's Third Dynasty, Djoser sought to align himself with eternity through the building of this structure. His ambitious plan for a monument to mark his burial, so expertly realized by his advisor and architect Imhotep, set the stage for the tradition of pyramid building that followed.

Djoser's burial vault was made of dressed granite laid in four courses, but the tomb was robbed during the ancient world, so by the time it was excavated in modern times, the body had long ago been removed. Undeterred, French architect Jean-Phillipe Lauer chose not just to excavate the area but also to reconstruct key portions of the 15-hectare sized complex surrounding the Step Pyramid.[69]

---

[68] Wilkinson, Toby. 2000. Royal Annals of Ancient Egypt. Routledge, USA. pp 79 & 258.

[69] Lauer, Jean-Phillipe. 1961. *The Pyramids of Sakkarah (Les Pyramides De Sakkarah)*. Imprimerie De L'Institut Graphique Egyptien, France.

**Reconstructed corridor leading to the entrance of the
Step Pyramid**

The whole design concept was on a level never seen or envisaged before. Historian Mark Van de Mieroop concluded, "Imhotep reproduced in stone what had been previously built of other materials. The facade of the enclosure wall had the same niches as the tombs of mud brick, the columns resembled bundles of reed and papyrus, and stone cylinders at the lintels of doorways represented rolled-up reed screens. Much experimentation was involved, which is especially clear in the construction of the pyramid in the center of the complex."[70] Indeed, tradition has it that Djoser was so pleased by Imhotep's work that he abandoned the convention that only the king's name appeared on his monuments and had Imhotep's name inscribed as well.[71]

Scholars disagree as to whether Imhotep served all four kings of the Third Dynasty, but evidence suggests he lived a long life. As he was so highly regarded, it seems unlikely that he did not serve pharaohs coming after Djoser as well. Whether under his direct supervision or not, Imhotep's innovations led to further developments of the pyramid later in the Third Dynasty. The landscape of Egypt was forever altered by the design of the Step Pyramid, and the rulers who followed Djoser were keen to put their own stamp on the landscape by proceeding with similar examples of monumental architecture. The next attempt occurred during the reign of the Pharaoh Sekhemkhet Djoserty. The second ruler of Egypt's Third Dynasty, Sekhemkhet Djoserty was Djoser's direct successor and has been estimated as ruling Egypt for approximately 6 years, with his own pyramid constructed sometime around 2645 B.C.[72]

---

[70] Van De Mieroop, 2010, p. 56
[71] Malek, 2002, p. 92-93
[72] Gardiner, Alan H. 1997. *The Royal Canon of Turin*. Griffith Institute, Oxford, UK.

The Pyramid of Sekhemkhet was of a grand design, located to the southwest of the Step Pyramid. Everything about its design suggests that the monument was envisaged to build upon the example of the first pyramid and surpass it both in scale and style. But unfortunately, possibly due to his period of reign being shorter to Djoser's, the Pyramid of Sekhemkhet was never actually completed. Far from dwarfing the Step Pyramid, the unfinished masterpiece instead barely progressed above ground level, earning it a less flattering nickname in the years to come: the Buried Pyramid. The fact that the Buried Pyramid literally did not get off the ground meant that it was not even discovered until the middle of the 20th century.

The unfinished Pyramid of Sekhemkhet

The next attempt at pyramid building also occurred during the Third Dynasty of Egypt. This was the Layer Pyramid, currently known locally in Arabic as the Round Pyramid. This structure was located in the necropolis of Zawyet el'Aryan in Egypt. Although still disputed, the Layer Pyramid has been argued as having contained the tomb of Khaba. Evidence for this comes not from the Layer Pyramid itself, but rather from excavations at a tomb inside the associated pyramid complex.

The Layer Pyramid

Archaeological excavation has uncovered a lot of data at both the Buried Pyramid and the Layer Pyramid. Excavations at the unfinished Pyramid of Sekhemkhet were undertaken in the 1950s by Egyptologist Zakaria Goneim. Prior to his archaeological investigation the pyramid was unknown, evidenced only by a strange rectangular shape in the desert. Goneim identified the pyramid as an unfinished structure consisting of one step measuring over 250 feet along its length. It was located in the middle of a larger complex, with a descending passageway on the northern side.[73] Through the passage, some Third Dynasty stone vessels and papyri were located, and a wooden casket containing gold was discovered, along with beads and jars inscribed with Sekhemkhet's name. An alabaster sarcophagus cut from a single block was also identified and revealed as empty after its opening, possibly due to the grave robbers of an earlier era. Egyptologist Jean-Philippe Lauer also located a partially destroyed tomb at the southern side of the Buried Pyramid with a wooden coffin containing the remains of a two-year old child.[74]

---

[73]Goneim, Zakaria. 2010. *The Lost Pyramid*. Rinehart & Company Inc, New York.

[74] Lauer, Jean-Phillipe. 1961. *The Pyramids of Sakkarah (Les Pyramides De Sakkarah)*. Imprimerie De L'Institut Graphique Egyptien, France.

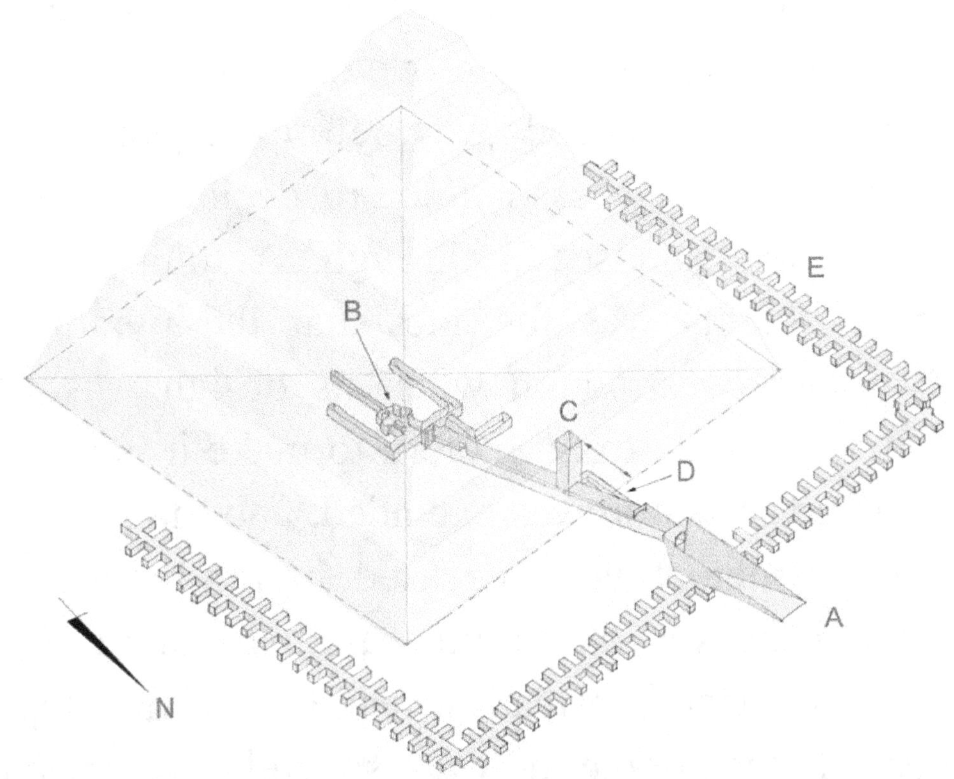

A computer generation of what's believed to be the intended design for the Buried Pyramid. Photo by Franck Monnier

At the end of the Third Dynasty, none of Egypt's rulers had yet been able to exceed the design of Imhotep and the ambition of Djoser as exemplified by the Step Pyramid. However, Pharaoh Huni was determined to succeed, so he ordered construction work to begin to the south of contemporary Cairo in Meidum (or Maidum). The town was to be the location of a large pyramid, which in turn would be surrounded by a cluster of huge mud-brick mastabas. Known later as the Pyramid of Meidum, this structure sought in its design to emulate the initial work of Imhotep, and its designer was even one of Imhotep's successors, but the successor's modifications to the initial Step Pyramid design were to prove disastrous.

The Pharaoh Huni passed away before the work could be completed, so his successor Sneferu decided to carry on with the works and see it through. Adding to already existing problems was the fact that the pyramid was already under construction when its design was altered due to new requests from Sneferu to make it bigger. As a result, the construction was extended, and the steps of the completed structure were encased in limestone upon a sand base. However, due to this sand base and a gradient on the outer surface, instead of resulting in flat steps, the stability of the pyramid was severely compromised. Before it reached completion, one of Egypt's rare storms led to a downpour that wreaked havoc upon this altered design, washing down the structure and eroding it to the point that the unfinished pyramid collapsed under its own weight. This unfortunate event led to a less than flattering nickname to be associated with the structure in later years: the Fake Pyramid.[75]

---

[75] Mendelssohn, Kurt. 1974. *The Riddle of the Pyramids*. Thames & Hudson, London.

The pyramid at Meidum

A mortuary temple at the pyramid

The so-called Fake Pyramid was abandoned at this point

and left incomplete. Its tomb remained empty, with raw walls and wooden support struts in place, and the mortuary temple of its base was covered by rubble and left there. Still, the Pharaoh Sneferu was not so easily deterred. Djoser's Step Pyramid had been an unqualified success, and Sneferu was intent on repeating the magic somehow. Around 2600 B.C., he commissioned another pyramid to be undertaken in the royal necropolis of Dahshur. Learning from the lessons of the collapsed Pyramid of Meidum, the angle of gradient to the pyramid's sides was altered during this attempt. It is also possible that early signs of instability caused a redesign during the construction phase, but either way, the alterations led to the pyramid's top section tapering in at a different angle to the base section of the structure. While the lower sections of the pyramid measured 52 degrees, the slope gradient of the pyramid's sides were altered to 43 degrees towards the top of this pyramid. This earned the structure its own disparaging title: the Bent Pyramid.[76]

---

[76] Verner, Miroslav. 2001. *The Pyramids - Their Archaeology and History*. Atlantic Books, USA.

Pictures of the Bent Pyramid

While the Bent Pyramid certainly looks strange, especially in comparison to Egypt's most famous pyramids, the significance of the Bent Pyramid is the way in which its design represents a transitional stage. The design of the Step Pyramid had been altered, and this was the first attempt to construct a smooth-sided pyramid. The result was not exactly as intended, but it was a new direction for pyramid designs in Egypt, and what it did achieve would be improved upon in the years to follow. It boasted two entrances, multiple chambers (including one below ground), and a hole in the ceiling of the northern chamber connecting to the western entrance's passage way. Two stone blocks covered this western entrance, sliding down ramps to block the passage. The pyramid, named at the time as Sneferu's Southern-Shining-Pyramid, to this day still retains the majority of its outer layer of polished limestone.[77]

While the Bent Pyramid certainly looks strange, especially in comparison to Egypt's most famous pyramids, the significance of the Bent Pyramid is the way in which its design represents a transitional stage. The design of the Step Pyramid had been altered, and this was the first attempt to construct a smooth-sided pyramid. The result was not exactly as intended, but it was a new direction for pyramid designs in Egypt, and what it did achieve would be improved upon in the years to follow. It boasted two entrances, multiple chambers (including one below ground), and a hole in the ceiling of the northern chamber connecting to the western entrance's passage way. Two stone blocks covered this western entrance, sliding down ramps to block the passage. The pyramid, named at the time as Sneferu's Southern-Shining-Pyramid, to this day still retains the majority of its outer layer of polished limestone.[78]

The Bent Pyramid revolutionized subsequent building techniques, but as any view of the pyramid quickly

---

[77] Verner, Miroslav. 2001. *The Pyramids - Their Archaeology and History*. Atlantic Books, USA
[78] Verner, Miroslav. 2001. *The Pyramids - Their Archaeology and History*. Atlantic Books, USA

indicates, all did not go as planned. Possibly dissatisfied at the end result for the Bent Pyramid, Pharaoh Sneferu started work immediately on a new structure adjacent to the last one. This time, the angle was corrected on this new pyramid to be 43 degrees from the very base of it, all the way to its apex. This would come to be called the Red Pyramid, based the red color of the stone used to construct it, or sometimes the North Pyramid. It is even referred to by locals occasionally as the Bat Pyramid.

The Red Pyramid. Photo by Ivrienen

The entry point into the Red Pyramid

A passageway inside the Red Pyramid

The name of the Red Pyramid was applied to it long after construction, because it was originally encased with white Tura limestone. Its underlying reddish color was only revealed over time as the limestone was stripped away, taken by builders who used it for their own local construction needs. Such works would include a variety of buildings in Cairo constructed during Egypt's so called

Middle Ages. Some instances of the past casing are still visible at the site, but by and large it is all gone, revealing the red color underneath. When this pyramid was completed, it broke a number of world records. It became the tallest standing human constructed structure anywhere in the world at that time, and it also became the first successful construction of a smooth-sided pyramid.[79]

Located less than a mile to the north of the Bent Pyramid, the Red Pyramid was a resounding success for Sneferu. He had redesigned the pyramid, coming up with a new look in the smooth sides. It was also a more stable structure, supported by the degree of gradient to the apex, which changed from 52 degrees to 43 degrees. How long it took to build is open to interpretation, with Egyptologist John Romer estimating 10 years and 7 months based on graffiti inscriptions found at the site.[80] Egyptologist Rainer Stadelmann estimates it took approximately 17 years to build.[81] It began in Pharaoh Sneferu's 30th year of reign, and by the time it was finished, it was the template for all the pyramids to follow, including the greatest of them all: the Great Pyramid of Giza.

Imhotep and the Step Pyramid's Legacy

There has been considerable academic research into why this particular dynasty witnessed such far-reaching

---

[79] Verner, Miroslav. 2001. *The Pyramids - Their Archaeology and History*. Atlantic Books, USA.

[80] Romer, John. 2012. *A History of Ancient Egypt: From the First Farmers to the Great Pyramid*. Allen Lane, USA.

[81] Die ägyptischen Pyramiden, vom Ziegelbau zum Weltwunder, Mayence, 1985–1997, éditions von Zabern (Kulturgeschichte der Antiken Welt, Bd. 30),

changes in religious practices, engineering, and the arts. Historians such as Douglas J. Brewer[82] suggest the answer lies in the specific pharaohs from the time, as well as the officials surrounding them. Djoser's reign was one of unusual stability, and it was the maintenance of this calm that enabled the creation and accumulation of wealth. In turn, this freed the pharaoh to have the resources and the time to embark on ambitious building projects.[83] Specifically, Djoser's military successes in the Sinai resulted in an unprecedented expansion of industry, which stimulated developments in technology and the arts.

Sekhemkhet is thought to have been Djoser's eldest son (or brother). He continued with Djoser's military campaigns after his succession and was able to maintain the stability enabling the Egyptian economy to continue to flourish. Khaba was the third king of the Third Dynasty (although there is the possibility that Sanakht ruled for a short time before Khaba came to the throne). Khaba's brief reign was followed by that of Huni, who was the last ruler of the Third Dynasty. He also continued the policies of his predecessors. What these pharaohs all had in common was the ability to maintain peace and order within the country through policies that stimulated the economy, creating the wealth that enabled the development of ideas in various aspects of life. It was in

---

[82] Brewer, 2014

[83] Indeed, the number of buildings, tombs, and temples is so large there is speculation that he ruled for a considerably longer period than 30 years (Manetho, *Aegyptiaca* (*History of Egypt*)).

this environment that Imhotep was able to influence ideas and practices.

Imhotep's design and the practical construction of the Step Pyramid is a prime example of the combination of opportunity and ability-bearing fruit. The Step Pyramid required its builders to think on a much larger scale than their predecessors. The old ways of building using mud-baked brick and wood were replaced by stone, and this single decision influenced Egyptian art and architecture for the next 2,000 years. Moreover, the technology required to move, shape, and position the stone required new and innovative thinking and the development of skills in working with stone which was not previously necessary.

Developments in religious concepts went hand-in-hand with these changes, especially in relation to the nature of the soul, and it was at this time that the concept of the soul having nine parts emerged.[84] Tradition has it that Imhotep was instrumental in directing these innovations and facilitating them. Though very little is known of him as a person, his name means "the one who comes in peace," and in addition to being Djoser's chief minister, he was high priest of the sun god Ra at Heliopolis. This position gave him enormous influence on religious practices.

Imhotep was an important figure in his own lifetime, and his impact on architecture is evidenced by his pyramids.

---

[84] Brewer, 2014; Van De Meiroop, 2010

However, it was in the centuries following his death that he became more revered and ultimately deified. His ideas were taken up and developed further, even though there are no extant primary texts from his lifetime that extol the skills and qualities ascribed to him in these later centuries, particularly in relation to his medical expertise.[85]

The first reference to Imhotep after the Third Dynasty period dates to the reign of Amenhotep III of the Eighteenth Dynasty, who ruled between 1391 B.C. and 1353 B.C.: "The wab-priest may give offerings to your ka. The wab-priests may stretch to you their arms with libations on the soil, as it is done for Imhotep with the remains of the water bowl."[86] The implication is that such libations to Imhotep had been on-going for some time. This assessment is confirmed by further references to the practice on papyri being associated with statues of Imhotep until the Late Period (664-332 B.C.). Wildung argues that a cult to Imhotep had evolved slowly among intellectuals right from his death. Such offerings to commoners were so unique that Alan Gardiner concluded Imhotep was venerated as semi-divine in the New Kingdom period.[87] The first references to Imhotep as a healer date from the Thirtieth Dynasty (around 380 B.C.), fully 2,000 years after his death.[88]

---

[85] Musso, 2005, p. 169
[86] Wildung, 1977, p. 34
[87] Hurry, 1926/2014, pp. 47-48
[88] Wildung, 1977, p. 44

The center of Imhotep's cult was in Memphis, but the location of his tomb is still unknown (but most likely to be within or near the complex at Saqqara). There is also a sanctuary at Hatshepsut's Deir el-Bahari in Thebes dedicated to him, and he is also represented in the temple at Deir-el-Medina.[89] The Banquet Song, written for a harper and inscribed on the walls of the Eighteenth Dynasty tomb of Paatenemheb in Saqqara includes: "I have heard the sayings of Imhotep and Djedefhor, / with whose utterances people discourse so much."[90]

Imhotep's historicity is confirmed by two contemporary inscriptions made during his lifetime (referred to above). The latter inscription indicates that Imhotep outlived Djoser but by how long is unknown.[91] As the chief official, Imhotep would have been ultimately responsible to the pharaoh for all major building projects, and as high priest, he would have either brought in changes he initiated or approved any proposals by others. In addition to his design of the first pyramids, he is also credited with being the first to use stone columns to support structures.[92]

Another aspect of Imhotep's later fame lay in his perceived wisdom as a philosopher, although there is no surviving text that can be definitively ascribed to him.

---

[89] Wilkinson, 2002

[90] Hirst, 2019

[91] Malek, 2002, pp. 92-93; Kahl, 2001, p. 592
[92] Baker and Baker, 2001, p. 23

However, a number of philosophical works, books of poetry, and treatises were attributed to him by later generations. By the time of the Middle Kingdom (1975 B.C.-1640 B.C.), he was regarded as the author of a pivotal book of instruction and was remembered as an important philosopher.[93] By the late New Kingdom, he had been named as one of was of the seven great ancient sages of the Egyptian world associated with literature.[94]

It was not until fully 2,000 years after his death that Imhotep was deified. With that, he was worshipped as a god of medicine and healing and was strongly equated with Thoth, the god of architecture, mathematics, and medicine.[95] Significantly, Thoth was also the patron of scribes and was said to be the scribe of the gods, as well as their main counselor. In this role, Thoth was thought to have invented writing and hieroglyphs.[96] He also had a role in the underworld as Aani, where he was the god of equilibrium, who carried out the weighing of the dead's hearts before they were presented to Osiris.[97]

The Egyptians believed Thoth to be the source of all works of science, religion, philosophy, and magic.[98] The

------

[93] Hirst, 2019,

[94] Hart, 2005

[95] Thoth's main temple was in Hermopolis where he was the leader of "the Ogdoad," a group of eight deities. The first references to the Ogdoad date to the Old Kingdom, and they are frequently mentioned in the *Coffin Texts* of the Middle Kingdom (see Salmon, 1887).

[96] Budge, 1904/1969, p. 414

[97] Budge, 1904/1969, p. 403

[98] Budge, 1904/1969, pp.401- 407

Greeks believed his sphere of influence even greater, attributing the invention of astronomy, astrology, the science of numbers, mathematics, geometry, surveying, medicine, botany, theology, civilized government, the alphabet, reading, writing, and oratory to him. Basically, he was the author of every work of every branch of knowledge, human and divine.[99] It is perhaps not surprising, then, that Thoth played numerous roles in Egyptian mythology, including maintaining the universe, and along with Ma'at, he traveled on Ra's barque.[100] As the god of wisdom, writing, hieroglyphs, science, magic, art, judgment, and the dead, the association of Imhotep the scribe, architect, and mathematician, is also clear. What is more perplexing is why the ancient Egyptians conflated the two. The process, no doubt, began with the practice of placing the cult of Imhotep in temples to Thoth.

The concept of Imhotep as a divine figure was strengthened by the miracles associated with him. One of these is a legend recorded on the Famine Stela.[101] The inscription records Egypt's suffering a terrible famine lasting seven years during Djoser's reign, which Imhotep was believed to have ended. Another 2nd century A.D. text recounts a tale from Djoser's reign that refers to Imhotep's family, stating that his father was the god Ptah, his mother Khereduankh, and his younger sister Renpetneferet.[102]

---

[99] Budge, 1904/1969, p. 414

[100] In Egyptian art, Thoth was depicted as a man with the head of a baboon.

[101] The inscription was found on Sehel Island in the Nile near Aswan (see Lichtheim, 2006).

The story claims that Djoser desired Renpetneferet but Imhotep magically disguised himself and rescued her from the king's clutches.

As one of the major instigators of innovation in Egyptian culture, Imhotep's reputation as an ideal counselor and sage lasted well into the Roman period, but his association with medicine came more and more to the fore. Egyptologist James Peter Allen noted that: "The Greeks equated him with their own god of medicine, Asklepios, although ironically there is no evidence that Imhotep himself was a physician."[103] A temple dedicated to Imhotep was built at Memphis around 600 B.C., which the Greeks called the Asklepion. Nearby, there also was a famous hospital and school of magic and medicine, which became an important center of pilgrimage for the ill and for childless couples. Greek physician Hippocrates is said to have been inspired by the books kept at the Asklepion temple.[104]

Despite Allen's assertion that there is no concrete evidence Imhotep was a physician, Imhotep's legend as a physician certainly dates from the Old Kingdom, and Imhotep's work as a medical scientist is potentially confirmed by the so-called Edwin Smith Papyrus.[105] This papyrus was found in a tomb in the mid-nineteenth

---

[102] Lichtheim, 2006, p. 106.
[103] Allen, 2005, p. 12
[104] Mark, 2016
[105] Named after Edwin Smith (1822-1906), an American collector of antiquities, who bought it in 1862.

century, measuring 15 feet in total length. Believed to be the oldest known surgical treatise, it outlines in considerable detail the treatment of 48 cases of trauma (listed according to each organ, with injuries to the head being dealt with first) and 100 diseases.[106] Each case identifies the nature of trauma and includes "[p]ractices for a gaping wound in the head, which has penetrated to the bone and split the skull."[107] The examination process as described is reminiscent of what any similar patient might expect today, including checking visual and olfactory clues, palpation, and the taking of the pulse.

The papyrus also includes quite accurate anatomical, physiological and pathological observations, and it is the first known description of cranial structures, the meninges, the external surface of the brain, cerebrospinal fluid, and intracranial pulsations. The level of knowledge of medicines is far advanced than that of Hippocrates, who lived 1,000 years later.[108] Indeed, the degree of detailed information has taken the modern medical world aback, including recognition of the influence of brain injuries on parts of the body and paralysis. The very detailed nature of the text has led some to conclude that it was a practical guidebook for those having to deal with injuries sustained in battle.[109] These works remained

---

[106] Nunn, 1996, *pp. 57–68*
[107] Allen, 2005, p. 74
[108] Ghalioungui, 1963/1965, p. 59.
[109] Allen, 2005, p. 11

popular in the Roman Empire, and in the temples of both Tiberius and Claudius, there are inscriptions praising Imhotep.

The Edwin Smith Papyrus is dated to 1600 B.C., but the text includes evidence that indicates it was a copy of a source first written around the time of Imhotep. This has led some to speculate that it may well have been written by Imhotep.[110] Whether it was or not, or even whether Imhotep was a practicing physician, is not of primary concern here. What is apparent is that Egyptians saw him as a doctor. There is very little reference to magic or spells that were so prevalent in other Egyptian medical texts. If Imhotep did write this treatise on disease and injury, which argued that they occurred naturally rather than being punishments sent by gods or inflicted by spirits or curses, he was well ahead of his time.

In commenting on Djoser's Step Pyramid, Miroslav Verner noted, "Few monuments hold a place in human history as significant as that of the Step Pyramid in Saqqara...It can be said without exaggeration that [Imhotep's] pyramid complex constitutes a milestone in the evolution of monumental stone architecture in Egypt and in the world as a whole. Here, limestone was first used on a large scale as a construction material, and here the idea of a monumental royal tomb in the form of a pyramid was first realized."[111] He went on to point out

---

[110] Breasted, 1930/1991, p. 9

that Imhotep had a vision "to build a colossal monument entirely of stone. He was able to imagine a feat never attempted before, perhaps never even conceived of, and make it a reality; in doing so, he changed the world. The great temples and administrative buildings, palaces and tombs, the majestic monuments of the pyramids and towering statuary which came to define the Egyptian landscape, all began with Imhotep's vision of the Step Pyramid at Saqqara. Once a monument built of stone had been accomplished, it could be attempted again, and then again with greater attention to detail and improvement in technology to create the "true pyramids" of Giza. Further, visitors to Egypt who saw these immense creations brought back reports of them to their own countries, such as Greece, who then built upon what Imhotep had first imagined and then made real."[112]

Related to the whole design of the Step Pyramid was the Egyptian religious obsession with preparations for the afterlife. As chief minister and high priest of Ra, Imhotep would have overseen the consolidation of belief in concepts of the soul and the nature of the underworld, ideas that formed the core of Egyptian religion for centuries to come. He also lived and operated in a particularly fortuitous time of peace and plenty, which allowed him and others to concentrate on ideas, practical

---

[111] Verner, 2002, pp. 108-109
[112] Verner, 2002, pp. 108-109

science, technology, and the arts.

It was during what might be termed Egypt's second "Golden Age" that he re-emerged as a key figure around whom intellectuals could coalesce as a symbol of willingness to innovate. His cult grew steadily in the centuries following his death, and he became more and more associated with medicine and the idea of the wise counselor. This association, combined with the practical siting of his worship in temples to Thoth, led to Imhotep's cult to ultimately merge with that of Thoth's. There can be no doubt that Imhotep was what might in more modern times be described as a "Renaissance Man," interested in all aspects of human life, practical yet artistic, detail-oriented yet spiritual, and his influence on Egypt should not be underplayed. Yet some 2,000 years after his death, it was as a deity and associated with medicine and good counsel that Imhotep's cult spread to Greece and Rome, and his whole reputation rose to such a level that he became one of only two commoners deified by the ancient Egyptians.

Online Resources

Other books about ancient history by Charles River Editors

Other books about the Step Pyramid on Amazon

Bibliography

Allen, J.P. (2005). *The Art of Medicine in ancient Egypt. Yale University Press.*

Amenta, A. (2002). *The Egyptian Tomb as a House of Life for the Afterlife. In: Egyptological Essays on State and Society, R. Pirelli (Ed.). Università degli studi di Napoli L'Orientale, Dipartimento di studi e ricerche su Africa e paesi arabi.*

Assmann, J. (2001). The Search for God in ancient Egypt, D. Lorton (Trans.). Cornell University Press.

Aton Hymn. (2009). *Encyclopedia Britannica.* https://www.britannica.com/topic/Aton-Hymn.

Badawy, A. (1966). Architecture in ancient Egypt and the Near East. MIT Press.

Baker R. and C. Baker. (2001). Ancient Egyptians: People of the Pyramids. Oxford University Press.

Bard, K.A. (2008). *An Introduction to the Archaeology of ancient Egypt.* Blackwell Publishing Ltd.

Barsanti, A. (1902). Ouverture de la pyramide de Zaouiet el-Aryân. *Annales du service des antiquités de l'Égypte,* Vol. 2. https://gallica.bnf.fr/ark:/12148/bpt6k5724454d.image.r=c opte.langFR.f101.pagination

Bonacker, W. (1950). The Egyptian "Book of the Two Ways." Imago Mundi, 7.

Breasted, J.H. (1930/1991). The Edwin Smith Surgical Papyrus: published in facsimile and hieroglyphic transliteration with translation and commentary in two volumes. University of Chicago Press.

Brewer, D.J. (2014). Ancient Egypt: *Foundations of a*

Civilization. Routledge.

Budge, E.A.W. (1901). *The Book of the Dead: An English Translation of the Chapters, Hymns, Etc., of the Theban Recension, with Introduction, Notes, Etc, Volume 1.* Open Court Publications.

Budge, E.A.W. (1904/1967). *Gods of the Egyptians* Vol. 1. Dover Publications.

Budge, E.A.W. (2013). Egyptian Ideas of the Afterlife. Courier Corporation.

Budge, W. (1954). Egyptian Religion: Egyptian Ideas of the Future Life. Bell Publishing Company.

Bunson, M. (1991). *The Encyclopedia of ancient Egypt.* Gramercy Books.

Clayton, P. (2006). *Chronicle of the Pharaohs.* Thames and Hudson Ltd.

Coogan, M.D. (2013). A Reader of Ancient Near Eastern Texts: Sources for the Study of the Old Testament, "Negative Confessions." *Oxford University Press.*

Cooney, K. (2010). Gender Transformation in Death: A Case Study of Coffins from Ramesside Period Egypt. *Near Eastern Archaeology, 73*(4).

Davis. B. The Future of the Past. *Scientific American, 277(2).*

Dodson, A. (2000). The Layer Pyramid of Zawiyet El-Aryan Its Layout and Context. *Journal of the American Research Center in Egypt,* Vol. 37.

Dunham, D. (1978). *Zawiyet el-Aryan—The Cemeteries*

Adjacent To The Layer Pyramid. Museum of Fine Art.

Fleming, F. and A. Lothian. (1997). *The Way to Eternity: Egyptian Myth*. Duncan Baird.

Ghalioungui, P. (1963/1965). *Magic and Medical Science in ancient Egypt*. Barnes & Noble.

Gardiner, A. (1964). *Egypt of the Pharaohs*. Oxford University Press

Goneim, Z. (1956). *The Lost* Pyramid. Reinhart & Company.

Hart, G. (2005). *The Routledge Dictionary of Egyptian Gods and Goddesses* (2nd ed.). Routledge.

Hirst, K.K. (2019). *Biography of Imhotep, ancient Egyptian Architect, Philosopher, God*. https://www.thoughtco.com/imhotep-4772346.

Hornung, E. (1999). *The ancient Egyptian Books of the Afterlife*. Cornell University Press.

Hurry, J.B. (1926/2014). *Imhotep: The Egyptian God of Medicine*. Oxford.

Kahl, J. (2001). Old Kingdom: Third Dynasty. In: *The Oxford Encyclopedia of ancient Egypt Vol. 2*, D.B. Redford (Ed.). Oxford University Press.

Lauer, J.P. (1962). *Histoire monumentale des pyramides d'Égypte. Volume 1: Les pyramides à degrés (IIIe Dynastie), Bibliothèque d'étude* vol. 39. Institut français d'archéologie orientale - Bibliothèque d'études.

Lehner, M. (1997). *The Complete Pyramids – Solving the Ancient Mysteries*. Thames & Hudson.

Lepsius, K.R. (2002). *Denkmäler aus Aegypten und Aethiopien*: http://edoc3.bibliothek.uni-halle.de/lepsius/

Lichtheim, M. (2006). Ancient Egyptian *Literature: The Late Period*. University of California Press.

Malek, J. (2002). The Old Kingdom. In: *The Oxford History of ancient Egypt,* I. Shaw (Ed.). Oxford University Press.

Maraglioglio, V. and C. Rinaldi. (1963). *L'architettura delle Piramidi Menfite II*. Rapallo.

Mark, J.J. (2016). *Imhotep. World History Encyclopedia.* https://www.ancient.eu/imhotep/

Mark, J.J. (2017). The Soul in ancient Egypt. *World History Encyclopedia.* https://www.ancient.eu/article/1023/the-soul-in-ancient-egypt/.

Musso, C.G. (2005). Imhotep: The Dean among the ancient Egyptian Physicians. *Humane Medicine 5*(1).

Nunn, J.F. (1996). Ancient Egyptian *Medicine. Transactions of the Medical Society of London, 113,*

Picardo, N.S. *"Semantic Homicide" and the So-called Reserve Heads: The Theme of Decapitation in Egyptian Funerary Religion and Some Implications for the Old Kingdom. Journal of the American Research Center in Egypt, 43.*

Pinch, G. (1994). *Magic in ancient Egypt*. British Museum Press.

Quirke, S. and S. Spencer. (1992). *The British Museum*

Book of ancient Egypt. Thames & Hudson.

Raven, M. J. (2005). Egyptian Concepts on the Orientation of the Human Body. *The Journal of Egyptian Archaeology, 91*(1), 37–53. https://doi.org/10.1177/030751330509100103.

Reisner, G.A., and C.S. Fisher (1911, December). The Work of the Harvard University—Museum of Fine Arts Egyptian Expedition (pyramid of Zawiyet el-Aryan). *Bulletin of the Museum of Fine Arts (BMFA) 9, Boston, No. 54 Vol. IX.* http://gizapyramids.org/static/pdf%20library/bmfa_pdfs/bmfa09_1911_54to59.pdf.

Salmon, G. (1887). *Ogdoad. In: A Dictionary of Christian Biography, Literature, Sects and Doctrines, Volume IV, W. Smith & H. Waces (Eds.). John Murray.*

Stadelmann, R. (2007). King Huni: His Monuments and His Place in the History of the Old Kingdom. In *The Archaeology and Art of ancient Egypt. Essays in Honor of David B. O'Connor*, Zahi A. Hawass, and Janet Richards (Eds.). Band II, Conceil Suprême des Antiquités de l'Égypte.

Taylor, J.H. (2001) Death and the Afterlife in ancient Egypt. University of Chicago Press.

Van De Mieroop, M. (2010). *A History of ancient Egypt.* Wiley-Blackwell.

Verner, M. (2002). *The Pyramids: The Mystery, Culture, and Science of Egypt's Great Monuments.* Grove Press.

Wildung, D. (1977). *Egyptian Saints: Deification in Pharaonic Egypt*. New York University Press.

Wilkinson, R.H. and Richard H. (2003). *The Complete Gods and Goddesses of ancient Egypt*. Thames & Hudson.

Free Books by Charles River Editors

We have brand new titles available for free most days of the week. To see which of our titles are currently free, [click on this link](#).

Discounted Books by Charles River Editors
We have titles at a discount price of just 99 cents everyday. To see which of our titles are currently 99 cents, click on this link.